Prepared in cooperation with the U.S. Fish and Wildlife Service

Effects of Prescribed Burning on Marsh-Elevation Change and the Risk of Wetland Loss

U.S. Department of the Interior
U.S. Geological Survey

U.S. Department of the Interior
KEN SALAZAR, Secretary

U.S. Geological Survey
Marcia K. McNutt, Director

U.S. Geological Survey, Reston, Virginia 2012

For product and ordering information:
World Wide Web: http://www.usgs.gov/pubprod
Telephone: 1-888-ASK-USGS

For more information on the USGS—the Federal source for science about the Earth,
its natural and living resources, natural hazards, and the environment:
World Wide Web: http://www.usgs.gov
Telephone: 1-888-ASK-USGS

Suggested citation:
McKee, K.L. and Grace, J.B., 2012, Effects of prescribed burning on marsh-elevation change
and the risk of wetland loss: U.S. Geological Survey Open-File Report 2012-1031, 51 p.

Cover: The McFaddin National Wildlife Refuge marsh during a prescribed burn; photograph by Tommy
McGinnis

Acknowledgments

This project was funded in part by the U.S. Geological Survey-Fish and Wildlife Service (USGS-FWS) Science Support Partnership (Project Number 05-R2-02). We acknowledge associate USGS investigators, Don Cahoon and Glenn Guntenspergen (Patuxent Wildlife Research Center) and FWS partners, Andy Loranger and Patrick Walther (Texas Chenier Plain National Wildlife Refuge Complex). We greatly appreciate the cooperation and support provided by the personnel at the McFaddin National Wildlife Refuge, including Craig Crenshaw, Doug Head, and Mike Nance. Several people assisted in installation of plots and SETs or in data collection: Heather Baldwin, Julia Cherry, Wes Cochran, Kari Cretini, Ada Diz, Andy From, Amber Hanna, Philippe Hensel, Jim Lynch, Tommy McGinnis, Amy Trahan, Ellen Travis, and William Vervaeke. We also appreciate the comments and suggestions of Connie Herndon, Beth Middleton, and Chris Swarzenski on earlier versions of this report.

Contents

Figures

Tables

Conversion Factors

SI to Inch/Pound

Multiply	By	To obtain
Length		
centimeter (cm)	0.3937	inch (in.)
millimeter (mm)	0.03937	inch (in.)
meter (m)	1.094	yard (yd)
Area		
square meter (m^2)	0.0002471	acre
hectare (ha)	2.471	acre
square millimeter (mm^2)	0.001550	square inch (in^2)
square meter (m^2)	10.76	square foot (ft^2)
Mass		
gram (g)	0.03527	ounce, avoirdupois (oz)
Energy		
millivolt (mV)	0.001	volt

-Temperature in degrees Celsius (°C) may be converted to degrees Fahrenheit (°F) as follows:

°F=(1.8×°C)+32

-Vertical coordinate information is referenced to North American Vertical Datum of 1988 (NAVD 88)

-Salinity is expressed in permille (‰) units, which is approximately equal to the grams of salt per kilogram of solution. In this study, salinity was determined based on the refractive index of the solution and converted to permille units by the instrument (refractometer).

Effects of Prescribed Burning on Marsh-Elevation Change and the Risk of Wetland Loss

By Karen L. McKee and James B. Grace

Abstract

Marsh-elevation change is the net effect of biophysical processes controlling inputs versus losses of soil volume. In many marshes, accumulation of organic matter is an important contributor to soil volume and vertical land building. In this study, we examined how prescribed burning, a common marsh-management practice, may affect elevation dynamics in the McFaddin National Wildlife Refuge, Texas by altering organic-matter accumulation. Experimental plots were established in a brackish marsh dominated by *Spartina patens*, a grass found throughout the Gulf of Mexico and Atlantic marshes. Experimental plots were subjected to burning and nutrient-addition treatments and monitored for 3.5 years (April 2005 – November 2008). Half of the plots were burned once in 2006; half of the plots were fertilized seasonally with nitrogen, phosphorus, and potassium. Before and after the burns, seasonal measurements were made of soil physicochemistry, vegetation structure, standing and fallen plant biomass, aboveground and belowground production, decomposition, and accretion and elevation change (measured with Surface Elevation Tables (SET)). Movements in different soil strata (surface, root zone, subroot zone) were evaluated to identify which processes were contributing to elevation change. Because several hurricanes occurred during the study period, we also assessed how these storms affected elevation change rates. The main findings of this study were as follows:

1

1. The main drivers of elevation change were accretion on the marsh surface and subsurface movement below the root zone, but the relative influence of these processes varied temporally. Prior to Hurricanes Gustav and Ike (September 2008), the main driver was subsurface movement; after the hurricane, both accretion and subsurface movement were important.

2. Prior to Hurricanes Gustav and Ike, rates of elevation gain and accretion above a marker horizon were higher in burned plots compared to nonburned plots, whereas nutrient addition had no detectable influence on elevation dynamics.

3. Burning decreased standing and fallen plant litter, reducing fuel load. Hurricanes Gustav and Ike also removed fallen litter from all plots.

4. Aboveground and belowground production rates varied annually but were unaffected by burning and nutrient treatments.

5. Decomposition (of a standard cellulose material) in upper soil layers was increased in burned plots but was unaffected by nutrient treatments.

6. Soil physicochemistry was unaffected by burning or nutrient treatments.

7. The elevation deficit (difference between rate of submergence and vertical land development) prior to hurricanes was less in burned plots (6.2 millimeters per year [mm yr^{-1}]) compared to nonburned plots (7.2 mm yr^{-1}).

8. Storm sediments delivered by Hurricane Ike raised elevations an average of 7.4 centimeters (cm), which countered an elevation deficit that had accrued over 11 years.

Our findings provide preliminary insights into elevation dynamics occurring in brackish marshes of the Texas Chenier Plain under prescribed fire management. The results of this study indicate that prescribed burning conducted at 3- to 5-year intervals is not likely to negatively impact the long-term sustainability of *S. patens*-dominated brackish marshes at McFaddin National Wildlife Refuge and may offset existing elevation deficits by ≈ 1 mm yr^{-1}. The primary drivers of elevation change varied in time and space, leading to a more complex situation in terms of predicting how disturbances may alter elevation trajectories. The potential effect of burning on elevation change in other marshes will depend on several site-specific factors, including geomorphic/ sedimentary setting, tide range, local rate of relative sea level rise, plant species composition, additional management practices (for example, for flood control), and disturbance types and frequency (for example, hurricanes or herbivore grazing). Increasing the scope of inference would require installation of SETs in replicate marshes undergoing different prescribed fire intervals and in different geomorphic settings (with different hurricane frequencies and/or different sedimentary settings). Multiple locations along the Gulf and Atlantic coasts where prescribed fire is used as a management tool could provide the appropriate setting for these installations.

Introduction

Global mean sea level has been increasing at a rate of 3.2 millimeters per year (mm yr^{-1}) since 1992 (based on satellite altimetry; Colorado Center for Astrodynamics Research, 2011), with predicted future rates due to global warming being at 6 mm yr^{-1} or more (Parry and others, 2007). Coastal marshes must keep pace with rising water levels or become submerged. Local subsidence rates may combine with eustatic rates of sea-level rise to cause even faster rates of inundation locally. Emergent vegetation not only accelerates mineral sediment deposition and vertical accretion (through baffling of sediment-laden water by plant shoots) (Morris and others, 2002), but also directly contributes organic matter to soil formation (Nyman and others, 1993; Nyman and others, 2006; McKee and others, 2007; Neubauer, 2008; McKee, 2011). In fact, habitat stability of many coastal wetlands in relation to sea level rise may be the result of a feedback relationship between environmental conditions and plant matter accumulation (Nyman and others, 2006; Mudd and others, 2009; McKee, 2011). In some cases, the decaying plant shoots and other organic detritus accumulate on the marsh surface, contributing to vertical accretion, but in many marshes and swamps, plant roots and shoot bases contribute to subsurface soil expansion (McKee and others, 2007; Cherry and others, 2009; Langley and others, 2009; McKee and Cherry, 2009; McKee, 2011).

Any factor that influences plant production or organic matter decomposition will alter the net amount of biomass that accumulates in the soil. From a few studies, scientists have inferred organic contributions to vertical accretion and soil expansion based on analysis of sediment cores (Turner and others, 2006; Sanders and others, 2008). Direct measurements of changes in accretion and elevation in relation to accumulation of organic matter (and processes that control it) are necessary, however, to understand and predict habitat stability (Neubauer, 2008; Mudd and others, 2009). For example, manipulation of nutrient availability in an oligotrophic mangrove ecosystem altered root production, which in turn caused a change in direction and magnitude of elevation change (McKee and others, 2007). Two additional studies have shown experimentally that increases in atmospheric CO_2 can accelerate elevation gain in some coastal marshes by stimulating belowground production and upward expansion of the soil surface (Cherry and others, 2009; Langley and others, 2009).

On the other hand, disturbance processes may cause negative effects on accumulation of organic matter. Biological agents that damage or remove vegetation include grazers such as geese, nutria, muskrat, and snails (Gauthier and others, 1995; Ford and Grace, 1998; Silliman and others, 2005). Physical processes include sediment or wrack burial, erosion or scouring, and fire (Guntenspergen and others, 1995; Nyman and Chabreck, 1995). Of particular concern are marsh management practices that may alter accumulation of soil organic matter and vulnerability to submergence. Prescribed burning is a common management practice used in coastal marshes to reduce hazardous buildup of fuel, enhance wildlife habitat or food sources, and promote rare or endangered species (Nyman and Chabreck, 1995). Burning may stimulate marsh productivity through release of nutrients or may alternatively cause a net loss of organic matter through direct combustion of peat and/or a change in the species composition or plant tissue chemistry, which affects community production or decomposition rates (Hackney and De La Cruz, 1977; Schmalzer and others, 1991; Nyman and Chabreck, 1995; Ford and Grace, 1998; Gabrey and Afton, 2001; Smith and others, 2001; Ponzio and others, 2004). Burning not only removes aboveground biomass but may also remove upper layers of peat that may have accumulated over long periods of time (Nyman and Chabreck 1995). Depending on burn frequency and intensity, however, plant biomass production could be stimulated without substantial loss of accumulated organic material (Nyman and Chabreck 1995).

Scope of Research

The goal of this cooperative research was to address an information need identified by managers at McFaddin National Wildlife Refuge (NWR): *Does the prescribed fire regime currently in use adversely affect marsh elevations and increase the risk of wetland loss?* This study experimentally investigated how fire management and nutrient addition (with and without fire) affected elevation dynamics in a brackish marsh dominated by *Spartina patens* (Ait.) Muhl (marshhay cordgrass), a grass found throughout Gulf of Mexico and Atlantic marshes. A prescribed burn was applied once during the study, after one year of preburn measurements. We hypothesized that burning and/or nutrient addition would alter the net accumulation of organic matter, which would affect the rate of soil elevation change. Because several hurricanes occurred during the study, we also assessed the relative impact of these storms in relation to experimental treatment effects. Thus, our research was aimed at addressing the following questions:

1.   What are the main drivers of elevation change and do they vary over time?

2.   Does burning or nutrient enrichment have a positive or negative effect on elevation change?

3.   To what extent do biotic processes (shoot or root production, decomposition) contribute to elevation change in the experimental marsh and how are they affected by burning and nutrient enrichment?

The information gained in this study will be useful in designing and planning future fire regimes and will provide insight into controls on accretion and elevation change in brackish marshes. Together with other studies of fire effects on marsh elevation (Cahoon and others, 2010), this work will lead to better management strategies for coastal wetlands nationwide.

Study Area

The study was conducted at the McFaddin NWR, a 23,843 ha area, which is part of the Texas Chenier Plain National Wildlife Refuge Complex. Chenier plain marshes are typically more stable than those in more rapidly subsiding areas, such as in deltaic areas, but are still subject to rising sea level. The current rate of relative sea level rise at Galveston Pier 21, TX (tide gauge ID 8771450, 1908-2010) is 6.3 mm yr^{-1} (NOAA, 2011). The McFaddin NWR contains extensive expanses of freshwater, brackish, and salt marsh. To maintain plant diversity in this system, several management techniques are used, including prescribed burns, grazing, water level management, and exotic species control. The site selected for this study was a brackish marsh located along a bayou within the McFaddin NWR (29° 41'41.47"N, 94° 04'04.85"W) (fig. 1). The dominant plant species was *S. patens* with minor occurrence of *Bolboschoenus robustus* (Pursh) Soják. At this site, a thin organic mat (< 1 m thick) overlies deeper sediments composed of compacted silt and clay. Brackish marshes, including the area used in this study, are burned at about 3-year intervals, usually at the end of the growing season.

Figure 1. Map of the study site at McFaddin National Wildlife Refuge (top panel) and views (lower panels) of an experimental plot through four seasons prior to the prescribed burn.

Experimental plots were established in April 2005, and measurements were made seasonally through November 2008. During the study period, a total of 18,653 ha in the Refuge were treated by prescribed fire, and another 12,701 ha were burned by wildfire (table 1). The marsh encompassing the experimental plots was burned once in 2006 (see below for details). Also, four major hurricanes occurred during the study, including Hurricanes Katrina (August 29, 2005), Rita (September 24, 2005), Gustav (September 1, 2008), and Ike (September 13, 2008).

Table 1.   Summary of area (in hectares) burned in McFaddin National Wildlife Refuge during the
study period.

Year	Wild	Prescribed
2005	7,998	6,359
2006	509	1,917
2007	2,613	10,369
2008	1,581	8
Total	12,701	18,653
Combined	31,354	

Experimental Design

The experimental design was completely randomized with a 2 x 2 factorial treatment arrangement. Two rows of eight plots each were established in the interior marsh ≈ 120 m from the bayou. The plots were positioned several meters apart to isolate treatment effects. The perimeter of each plot (5.2 m x 3.2 m) was defined by a wooden platform that facilitated access and minimized disturbance (fig. 2). An extendible plank was laid across the platform to provide access to the plot interior. The plots were each divided into a section for nondestructive measurements and another section for destructive sampling (fig. 3).

Within the nondestructive segment of the plots, a rod surface elevation table (hereafter, SET) along with deep and shallow benchmarks and marker horizons were installed (see below for details) (fig. 3). Destructive measurements, including aboveground and belowground production, decomposition, and physicochemistry, were made in the other half of the plot (see below for details) (fig. 3).

Plots were randomly assigned to a nutrient treatment (none, nutrient addition) and a fire treatment protocol (burned, nonburned). Each nutrient-fire treatment combination was replicated four times for a total of 16 experimental plots (M1-16). Fertilized plots received a slow-release fertilizer (Vigoro Tree, Shrub, and Evergreen Food; Spectrum Brands; Madison, WI, USA; containing a 16:4:8 ratio of nitrogen, phosphorus, and potassium), which was broadcast onto the marsh surface during low water levels 3 times per year. The fertilizer treatment was initiated in April 2005 and continued until the end of the study in 2008.

The prescribed burn occurred on December 3, 2006 (fig. 4). Fire crews burned the surrounding marsh and allowed the fire to move across the study area. In preparation for the burn, platforms in burn plots were partially disassembled, and lumber was stored in adjacent (nonburned) plots. Deep and shallow benchmarks were protected by fire blankets. Half of the plots were prevented from burning by operation of a sprinkler system installed prior to the fire. The sprinkler system protected all but one nonburned plot where the sprinklers failed; this plot was partially burned. Temperature loggers were deployed in all burn plots and at three points in the surrounding marsh and retrieved after the burn. Surface temperatures reached a peak of 274° C in the marsh just northwest of the site; the maximum temperature in burn plots ranged from 32 to 185 ° C (fig. 5).

Figure 2.   Setup of experimental plots. Clockwise from top left: (1) construction of platforms, (2) study plot demarcated by access platform, (3) driving benchmark rods for installation of surface elevation tables (SET), (4) SET receiver cemented to deep benchmark rod.

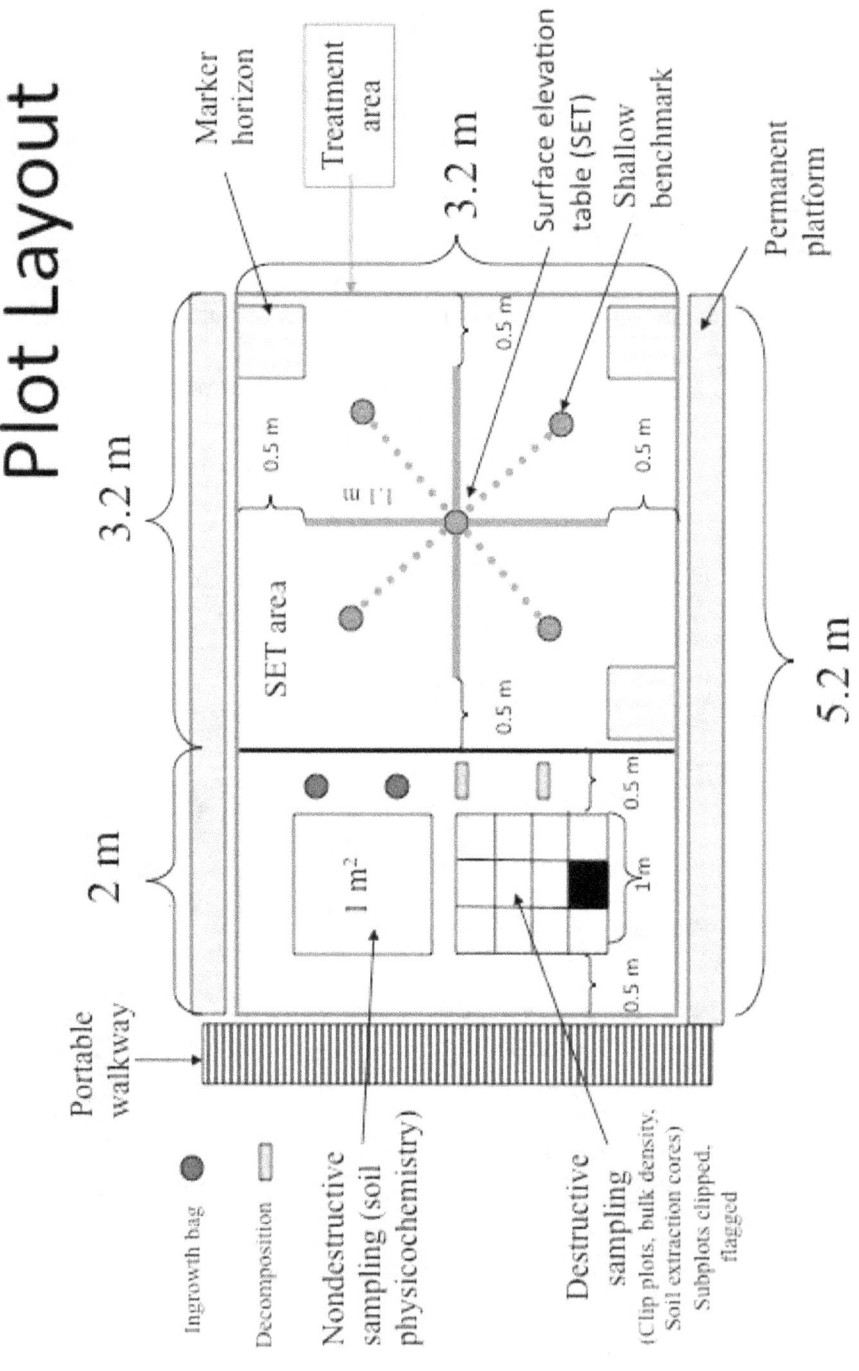

Figure 3. Schematic diagram of experimental plot showing positions of various measurements made during the study.

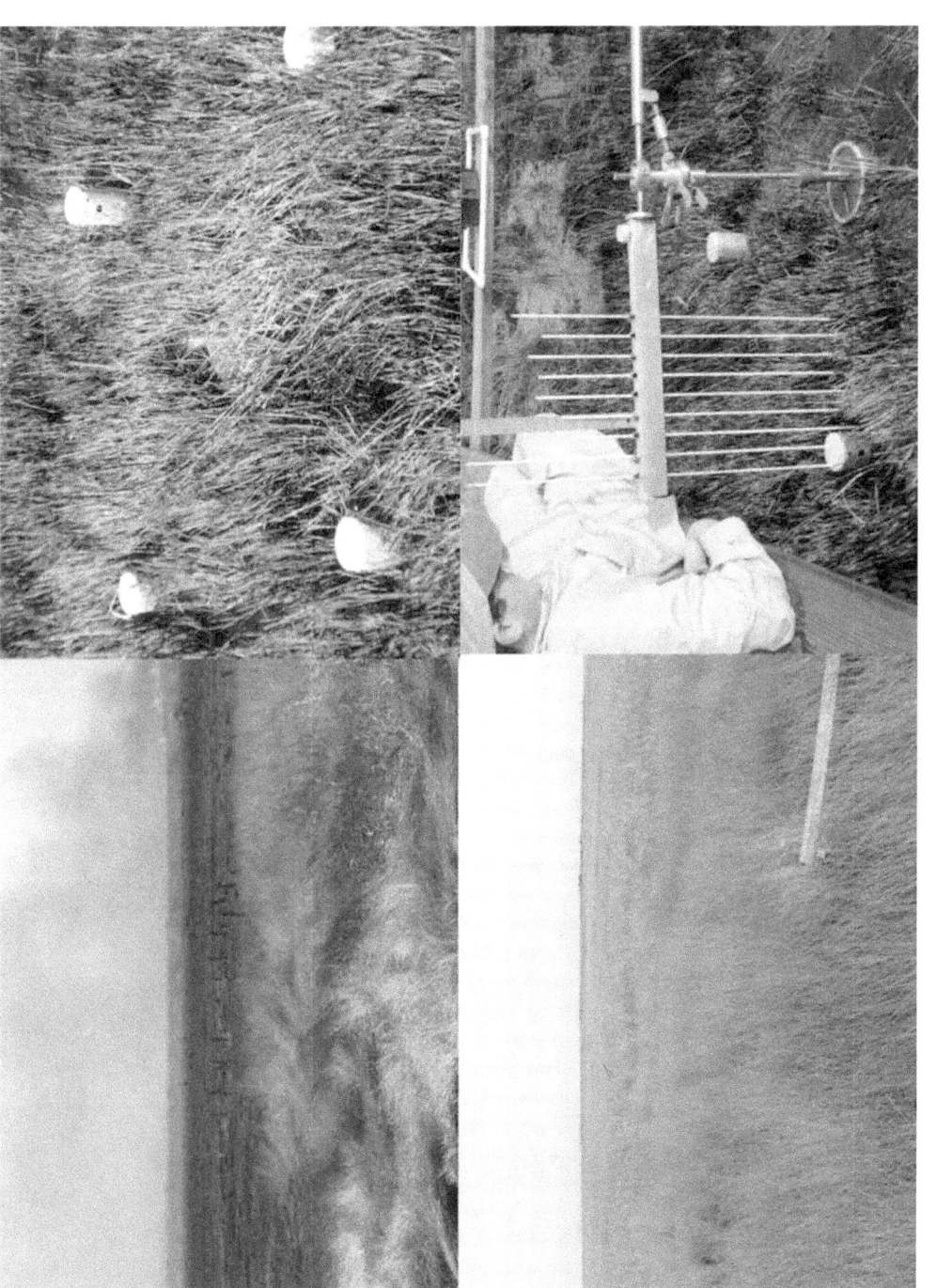

Figure 4. Views of study area during and after burn treatment (December 2006). Clockwise from top left: (1) prescribed burn, (2) initial plant regrowth after burn, (3) elevation measurement after burn treatment, (4) plant regrowth in spring 2007.

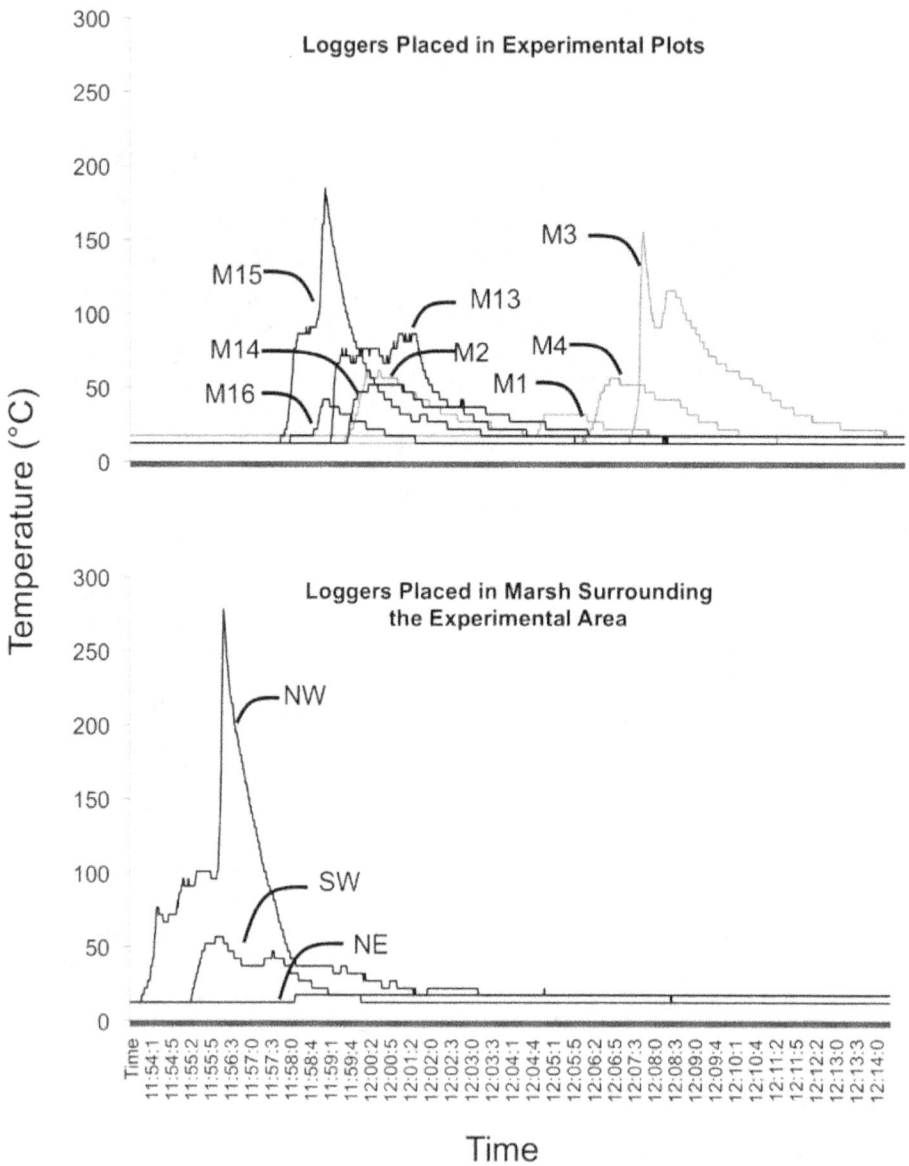

Figure 5.   Surface temperatures recorded by data loggers during the prescribed burn on

December 3, 2006. The upper panel shows data for experimental plots M13-16 (black lines)

and M1-4 (gray lines). The lower panel shows data for the surrounding marsh to the northwest

(NW), southwest (SW) and northeast (NE) of the plots.

Methods

Measuring Elevation Dynamics

Surface elevation change in each plot was determined to the nearest millimeter with SETs (Cahoon and others, 2002). Change in the elevation of the soil surface relative to the base of a benchmark reflects expansion or contraction over different portions of the sediment profile (fig. 6). The rod SET setup consisted of a benchmark rod driven to the point of refusal, four shallow benchmarks (30 cm deep), and a portable measuring arm. Deep benchmark rods were driven with a slide-hammer to depths of 15 to 16 m. Shallow benchmarks, which were constructed of 5-cm diameter x 40-cm long aluminum pipe capped at the top with an acrylic disc, were inserted into the soil to a 30-cm depth. During measurements, the portable arm was attached to the deep benchmark in one of four fixed directions and leveled in both horizontal and vertical planes. On each sampling date, seven fiberglass pins were lowered to the soil surface, and the extension distances above the arm were recorded. Changes in pin extension distance corresponded to changes in soil elevation relative to the baseline measurement. Two pins were lowered to the top of the shallow benchmark, which allowed movement in the root zone to be isolated from movement in the sub-root zone by partitioning change in the upper 30 cm from the total elevation change over the entire soil profile (figs. 6-7). Accretion of sediment on the soil surface was determined by using marker horizons (3 per plot) of white feldspar clay sown onto the soil surface (fig. 7). Marker horizons were $\approx$ 1 cm thick and covered an area of 0.25 m^2. Accumulation of sediment was determined at 4-month intervals by collecting cryogenic cores through each marker horizon (fig. 7) (Cahoon and others, 1996).

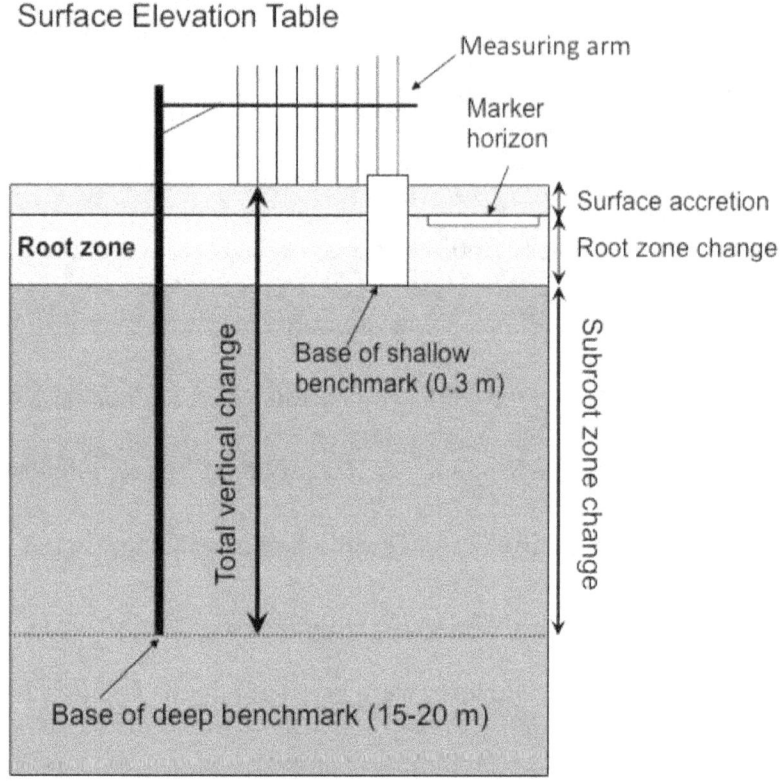

Figure 6. Diagram showing the rod surface elevation table (SET) in relation to deep and shallow benchmarks and marker horizon, which demarcate three strata in the soil profile to allow vertical delineation of processes controlling elevation change.

The marker horizon depth was measured at four positions around the core to the nearest millimeter and averaged. For each SET, a total of 28 deep-benchmark, 8 shallow-benchmark, and 3 marker-horizon measurements were recorded.

The elevations of the marsh surface in each SET plot were determined by using real-time kinematic (RTK) Global Positioning System measurements, with a minimum of 15-second (s) observations at four points within each plot. RTK elevations were expressed with respect to the North American Vertical Datum of 1988 (NAVD88).

Figure 7. Methods used to measure elevation change, accretion, subsidence, and root zone movement. Clockwise from top left: (1) Adding feldspar clay to soil surface to create a marker horizon, (2) Measuring thickness of accreted sediment above the marker horizon, (3) measuring arm of the surface elevation table being attached to the deep benchmark rod, (4) Fiberglass pins being lowered to the soil surface and to the shallow benchmark (white cap).

Measuring Aboveground and Belowground Plant Responses

Standing plant biomass was harvested at 4-month intervals by clipping all shoots at the soil surface within a 0.1-square meter (m^2) circular quadrat (fig. 8). All fallen litter was collected within the quadrat and bagged separately. Clipped plots were randomly selected from a gridded area and marked to avoid resampling. Standing and fallen material was later sorted by species and condition (live, dead), oven-dried (60° C), and weighed. Annual aboveground production was estimated by summing end-of-growing season standing live and dead biomass (Morris, 2007).

Belowground accumulation of roots and rhizomes was determined by using the in-growth method (McKee and others, 2007). Duplicate in-growth bags (5-cm diameter x 30-cm length) containing a root-free, standardized organic substrate (milled sphagnum peat) were installed in all plots at the beginning of the study (fig. 8). The bags were constructed of a flexible, large-mesh material (3 square millimeters (mm^2), J&M Industries, Ponchatoula, LA, USA), which allowed in-growth of both fine and coarse roots. A core of soil was removed initially, and a prefilled bag was inserted into the hole; the top of the bag was secured with twine to a stake. Bags were retrieved after one year by recoring; new bags were installed in the same location. Bags with ingrown material were divided into 10-cm segments, placed into ziplock bags, and kept cool until processing. All ingrown material was washed over a 1-mm sieve, separated into size classes (fine roots [<2 mm], coarse roots [>2 mm, rhizomes]) and condition [live or dead based on appearance and flotation], dried at 60 °C, and weighed. Rates of belowground production (to a 30-cm depth) were calculated by dividing the mass per unit area by the time interval to give an annual value (grams per square meter per year [g m^{-2} yr^{-1}]).

Figure 8.   Methods used to measure response to treatments.Clockwise from top left: (1) clipping

of aboveground biomass and litter collection, (2) collection of porewater for measurement of

salinity, pH, sulfide and nutrients, (3) installation of in-growth bags to measure rates of

belowground accumulation of root matter, (4) installation of a standardized cellulose material to

measure decomposition rates.

Measuring Decomposition

Decomposition rates in each experimental plot were measured by using the

"cotton-strip technique" (Slocum and others, 2009). Canvas material (100 percent undyed cotton, style number 568, Tara Materials, Inc., Lawrenceville, Ga.,

www.taramaterials.com) was cut into strips (10 cm x 30 cm) and inserted vertically into

the soil with a spade so that about 4 cm extended above the soil surface (fig. 8). The exact

position of the soil surface was marked by clipping a notch in the strip. Samples remained

in the ground for 10 days and then were retrieved; at the time of sample retrieval,

reference strips were inserted and immediately removed. At the laboratory, all strips were

washed with deionized water, air-dried, and stored away from sunlight. Sampling depths

were marked with a pencil on each strip and then sub-strips were cut by using a rotary

blade. Tensile strength of each sub-strip was measured with a tensometer (Slocum and

others, 2009). Rates of loss of cotton tensile strength were calculated as CTSL (%) = [1-

(N/C)/D] x 100, where N is the strength of the experimental sub-strip in Newtons; C is

the mean tensile strength of the reference sub-strips; and D is the number of days in the

ground.

Assessing Physicochemical Conditions

Duplicate samples of pore water were collected at a 25-cm depth in the

undisturbed section of the plot and analyzed for salinity, pH, sulfide, and nutrients as

described previously (McKee and others, 1988; McKee and McGinnis, 2002) (fig. 8).

Soil samples were collected with a piston corer for measurement of bulk density (dry

mass per volume) and percent organic matter (loss on ignition) according to standard

methods (Parent and Caron, 1993). Soil redox potentials at 1-, 15-, and 30-cm depths

were measured with bright platinum electrodes equilibrated in situ for 30 min (McKee

and others, 1988). Each electrode was checked before use with quinhydrone in pH 4 and

7 buffers (millivolt [mV] reading for quinhydrone is 218 and 40.8, respectively, at 25 C).

The potential of the calomel reference electrode (+244 mV) was added to each reading to calculate redox potential (Eh).

Performing Statistical Analyses

The elevation data (total change and vertical movement of each depth interval) were divided into the period prior to and after Hurricanes Gustav and Ike (September 2008) and analyzed separately. The total vertical departure (cumulative) from the baseline for each fiberglass pin (36 per SET) was calculated for each sampling date. The cumulative changes for the 28 pins lowered to the soil surface were averaged to provide an overall rate of mean elevation change (relative to the base of the deep benchmark) per SET per date. Similarly, the cumulative changes for the 8 pins lowered to the shallow benchmarks (4 directions per SET) were averaged and represented the movement between the base of the shallow benchmarks to the depth of the deep benchmark. The depths of sediment accreted above the three marker horizons per SET were also averaged to provide a single mean value for each SET per sampling date. Movement within the root zone was calculated by subtracting the shallow benchmark movement and accretion from total elevation change. Total subsurface change (subsidence or expansion) was calculated by subtracting accretion (above the marker horizon) from total elevation change (soil surface movement relative to the base of the deep benchmark). Thus, each SET plot provided five linear trajectories representing total elevation change, shallow subsidence, and movement in three strata, including surface accretion, root zone, and subroot zone. The slopes of these linear relationships were determined to provide a rate of change for each SET, which was considered to be the experimental unit.

Rates of change for elevation variables were analyzed by analysis of covariance (ANCOVA) using the NAVD88 elevation of the SET plots as a covariate and burn and fertilizer treatments as categorical grouping factors. Other variables (biomass and production) were analyzed by using a repeated-measures analysis of variance (ANOVA) with burn and nutrient treatments as grouping factors and time as the repeated measure. Decomposition data were assessed with repeated measures ANOVA by using burn and nutrient treatments as the grouping factors and depth as the repeated measure. If necessary, data were log-transformed to meet assumptions of ANOVA. Statistical analyses were performed with JMP® Version 9.0.0 (SAS Institute, Inc., Cary, N.C.).

Results and Discussion

Several considerations must be kept in mind when interpreting the results of this study. First, the study was conducted in one location within the McFaddin NWR and in one marsh habitat. Thus, the results may not be applicable to other locations or marsh types within the refuge or in other geographic locations, especially where conditions (for example, subsidence) are considerably different. Nevertheless, the natural mechanisms involved in controlling elevation dynamics in the experimental plots and the effects of burning and nutrient treatments on these mechanisms are generally relevant to other coastal marshes. Second, the responses to treatments do not necessarily indicate long-term responses to burning or nutrient treatments and, therefore, cannot be extrapolated beyond the time interval of the study. Third, these results reflect the effect of a single prescribed burn (simulating a 3- to 5-year burn interval); more frequent (annual) burning may produce different results. Fourth, several hurricanes occurred during the study and apparently influenced some of the response variables, including biomass accumulation, soil chemistry, and elevation dynamics.

With these caveats in mind, we describe the key results and their implications in the following sections.

1. **Result:** The main drivers of elevation change in the brackish marsh studied at McFaddin NWR were accretion on the marsh surface and subsurface movement below the root zone, but the relative influence of these processes varied temporally (with hurricane occurrence).

Movements in different soil strata contribute to elevation change of the marsh surface (Cherry and others, 2009; McKee and Cherry, 2009; McKee, 2011). Several biological and physical processes control these movements by promoting vertical expansion or contraction of these soil strata. Mineral and/or organic detritus is deposited on the soil surface and can undergo subsequent compaction or erosion or microbial decomposition (organic). Root-zone movement is driven by belowground production of roots, rhizomes, and shoot bases; decomposition of organic matter; and physical compaction. Below the root zone, subsidence and shrink-swell of the substrate (due to changing water content) predominate. The relative contribution of these processes in each soil strata varies among marshes and over time. This study quantified the rate and direction of movement in each of these soil strata, which allowed identification of the main processes controlling elevation change in the study site at McFaddin NWR.

Elevation and accretion in burned and nonburned plots varied over time relative to the initial baseline (fig. 9). Prior to Hurricanes Gustav and Ike, the rate of elevation change varied across all experimental plots from -9.1 to 7.9 mm yr^{-1}, with an overall average of -0.4 mm yr^{-1}. Elevation change was positively correlated with plot elevation, which varied from 0.235 to 0.301 m (NAVD88) (r = 0.71, P = 0.0021). This correlation likely reflects a feedback relationship between elevation and flooding-related factors influencing sedimentation and production-decomposition processes (Neubauer, 2008; Mudd and others, 2009; McKee, 2011). Accretion above marker horizons varied from 0.4 to 7 mm yr^{-1}, with an overall average of 3.2 mm yr^{-1}. Accretion exceeded elevation change throughout the 3.5 year observation period, indicating that subsidence was contributing to vertical movement of all plots regardless of treatment. The rate of average shallow subsidence across the study site was -3.6 mm yr^{-1}. The rate of shallow subsidence plus relative sea level rise (SLR) (6.3 mm yr^{-1}) yields a total submergence rate of 9.9 mm yr^{-1}. Vertical change in the root zone varied from -0.6 to 0.9 mm yr^{-1} (average = 0.2 mm yr^{-1}), indicating a slight, but overall expansion. Total elevation gain (accretion plus root zone) was 3.4 mm yr^{-1}. Thus, there was an overall elevation deficit (submergence minus elevation gain) of 6.5 mm yr^{-1} at this site prior to the 2008 hurricanes.

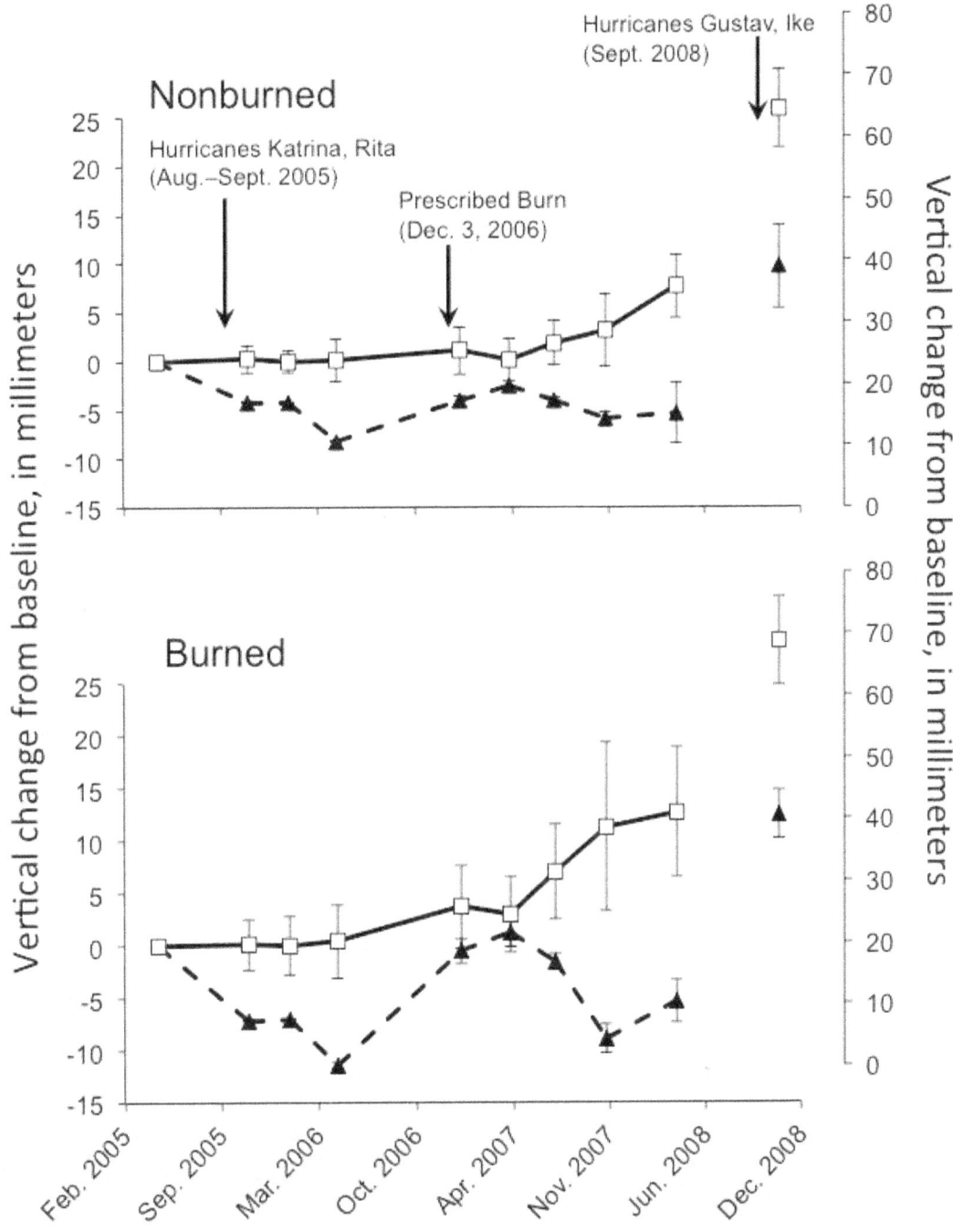

Figure 9. Time-course of elevation change (σ) and accretion above marker horizon (θ) in

nonburned and burned plots (mean ± standard error, n = 8, averaged over nutrient treatment).

Note different scales for Y-axis before (left) and after (right) Hurricanes Gustav and Ike.

To determine which processes were driving vertical movement of the marsh surface, elevation change rates across plots were assessed in relation to movement in the three main strata (surface, root zone, subroot zone) (fig. 10). Prior to Hurricanes Gustav and Ike, the primary driver of change was sub-root zone movement ($r = 0.92$, $P < 0.0001$). Movement below the root zone thus explained 85 percent of the variation in elevation change before this hurricane, whereas accretion and root zone expansion together explained only 15 percent. The storm surge associated with Hurricane Ike (East and others, 2008) delivered substantial sediment to experimental plots, which strongly influenced elevations (fig. 9). After this hurricane, accretion explained 53 percent and subroot zone movement explained 46 percent of the variation in elevation change (fig. 10). In Louisiana brackish marshes impacted by Hurricane Katrina, storm sediments also increased elevations by several centimeters, but post-hurricane elevation movement in upper soil layers was determined by the texture (for example, particle size and organic matter content) of the deposited sediment (McKee and Cherry, 2009).

Authors of a companion fire study conducted at Blackwater NWR (on the eastern shore of Maryland) found that marsh-elevation change, averaging 4 mm yr^{-1} across treatment plots, was driven by three main factors, including accretion, root-zone subsidence, and shrink-swell of sediments below the root zone (Cahoon et al. 2010). At Blackwater NWR, surface accretion was higher (5.9 – 9.7 mm yr^{-1}) and caused by litter accumulation rather than mineral sedimentation, but there was root-zone collapse (<-1 to -6 mm yr^{-1}). Overall, shallow subsidence varied from -1.7 to 5.9 mm yr-^{1}.

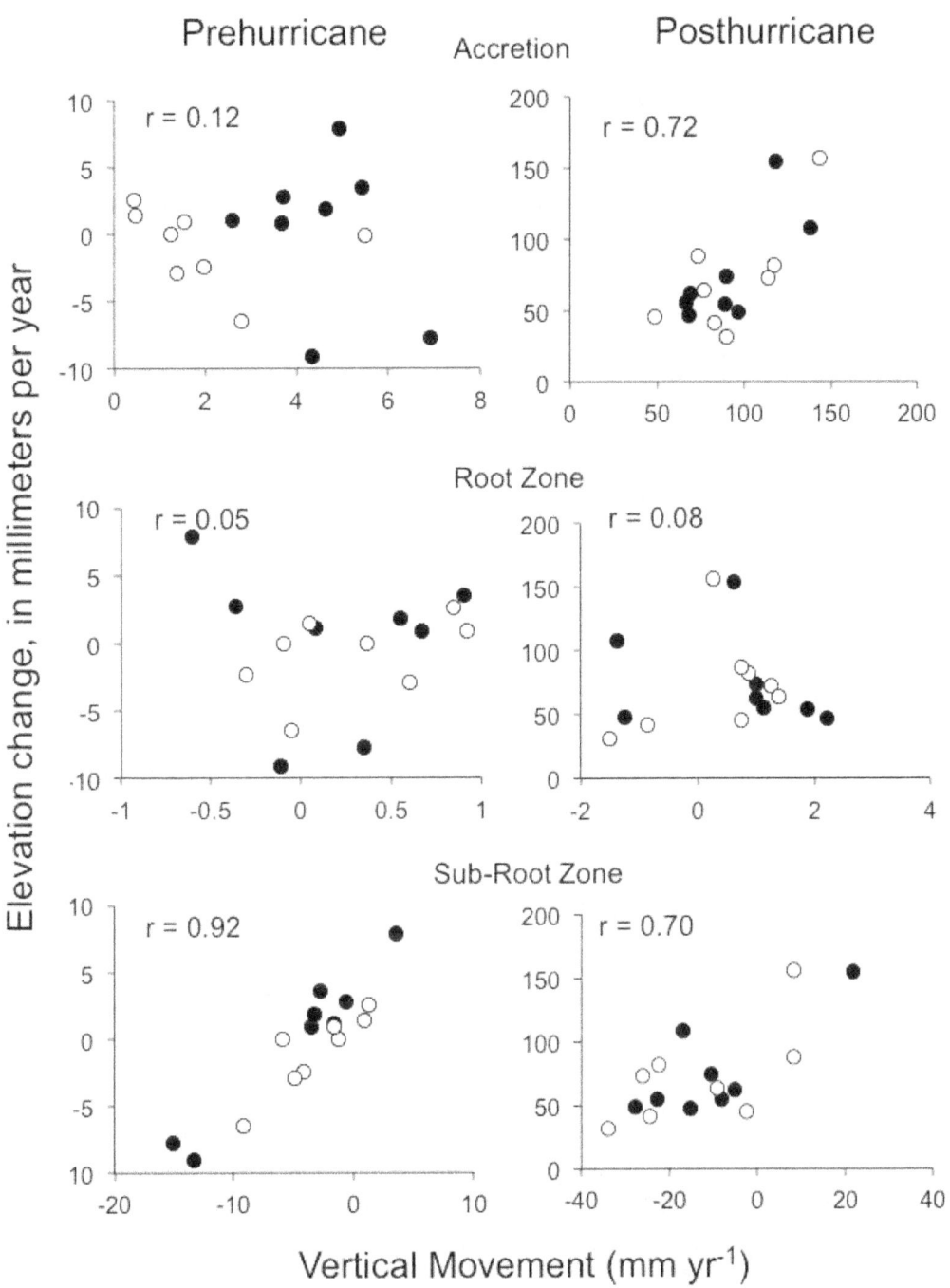

Figure 10. Variation in elevation-change rate (Y-axis) in relation to vertical movement (X-axis) in three strata, including accretion (top panels), root zone (middle panels), and subroot zone (bottom panels). Rates of change measured before and after Hurricane Ike (September 9, 2008) are plotted in left or right panels, respectively. Treatment plots are indicated by closed (burned) or open (nonburned) symbols. Inset values are correlation coefficients.

These results illustrate how relative movement in different soil strata (and associated processes) can vary substantially within and among marshes over time. Consequently, it is important to avoid viewing such controlling factors as static, either in time or space.

2. **Result:** Burn treatment increased rates of elevation gain and accretion compared to those in nonburned plots, whereas nutrient treatment had no detectable influence on elevation dynamics.

Because of the overriding effect of storm sediment on elevation dynamics, effects of fire and nutrient treatments were assessed by using data collected prior to the 2008 hurricanes (earlier hurricanes had no detectable effect). Before the 2008 hurricanes, nutrient addition did not significantly affect elevation-change rates, but burning had a significant effect on both accretion and elevation change. The burned plots gained elevation (+0.14 mm yr^{-1}), whereas nonburned plots lost elevation (-0.87 mm yr^{-1}) (main effect of fire, F = 5.34, P = 0.0496) (fig. 9). Thus, burning not only affected the magnitude of elevation change, but also the direction, and the difference caused by burning was approximately 1 mm yr^{-1}. Accretion above feldspar marker horizons also was higher in burned (4.5 mm yr^{-1}) compared to nonburned (1.9 mm yr^{-1}) plots. Sub-surface change indicated that some plots were subsiding, whereas others were undergoing expansion, but there was no effect of burning or nutrient treatments on root zone or subroot zone movement. These findings indicate that the effect of burning on soil expansion occurred in the surface layers (above the marker horizon). This effect may result from deposition of residual ash from the burned plant material that was deposited on the soil surface. The lack of a nutrient effect on elevation further suggests that burning mainly acted by causing a physical contribution to vertical accretion, rather than through stimulation of plant growth, such as roots on the marsh surface.

Similarly, a previous study conducted at McFaddin NWR found that marsh burning slowed the rate of elevation loss compared to a nonburned marsh after hurricane-induced flooding killed *S. patens* (the dominant vegetation), causing root zone collapse (Cahoon and others, 2004). The positive effect of burning appeared to be related to increased root growth resulting in an increase in organic matter volume, but effects on decomposition could not be ruled out. Results of the study at Blackwater NWR indicated no effect of burning on elevation change (Cahoon et al. 2010). Although not significantly different, there was a trend for faster accretion with decreasing burn frequency. Rates of accretion in marshes with different fire (frequency) regimes were 5.9 mm yr^{-1} (annual), 6.9 mm yr^{-1} (3–5 year), 8.4 mm yr^{-1} (7–10-year), and 9.7 mm yr^{-1} (control). Shallow subsidence tended to be slower in annually burned marshes (1.7 mm yr^{-1}) compared to control marshes (5.9 mm yr^{-1}) or plots undergoing burn frequencies of 3–5 year (3.4 mm yr^{-1}) and 7–10 year (3.3 mm yr^{-1}). Lower litter and accretion on the marsh surface may have offset root-zone subsidence, leading to similar rates of elevation change in annually burned marshes (4.0 mm yr-1), in marshes burned at other frequencies (3.9 mm yr^{-1} [3–5 year], 5.0 mm yr^{-1} [7–10 year]), and in control marshes (3.8 mm yr^{-1}).

3. Result: Burning decreased standing and fallen plant litter, reducing fuel load; Hurricanes Gustav and Ike also removed fallen litter from all plots.

Aboveground biomass (live and dead standing and fallen litter) varied over time and in response to burn and nutrient treatments and to hurricane impact (fig. 11). Aboveground live biomass was increased by nutrient addition before the prescribed burn (479 vs. 715 grams per square meter [$g\ m^{-2}$] in control and fertilized plots) but it did not differ among treatment and control plots after the burn and averaged 516 $g\ m^{-2}$ (time by nutrient interaction, $F = 6.8$, $P = 0.012$). Prior to the prescribed burn, standing dead biomass averaged 703 $g\ m^{-2}$ in subsequently burned and 841 $g\ m^{-2}$ in nonburned plots; litter averaged 181 $g\ m^{-2}$ in subsequently burned and 164 $g\ m^{-2}$ in nonburned plots. After the burn, dead biomass was significantly lower in burned (326 $g\ m^{-2}$, standing dead; 112 $g\ m^{-2}$, litter) compared to nonburned (736 $g\ m^{-2}$, standing dead; 365 $g\ m^{-2}$, litter) plots. After Hurricanes Gustav and Ike, litter in all plots was decreased to approximately 51 $g\ m^{-2}$ and did not differ among burn and nutrient treatments. At Blackwater NWR, annual burning led to lower standing dead biomass (38 $g\ m^{-2}\ yr^{-1}$) compared to less frequently burned marshes (175–216 $g\ m^{-2}\ yr^{-1}$ (Cahoon et al. 2010).

Live and dead stem densities also varied over time and in response to burning (fig. 12). Prior to the burn, live stem density was similar in subsequently burned (1021 stems m^{-2}) and nonburned (964 stems m^{-2}) plots; after the burn, density was two times higher in burned (2309 stems m^{-2}) than in nonburned (1054 stems m^{-2}) plots (fire by time interaction, $F = 5.38$, $P = 0.0235$). Live density decreased to zero after Hurricanes Gustav and Ike. Dead stem density varied over time, but differences between burned and nonburned plots were not significant.

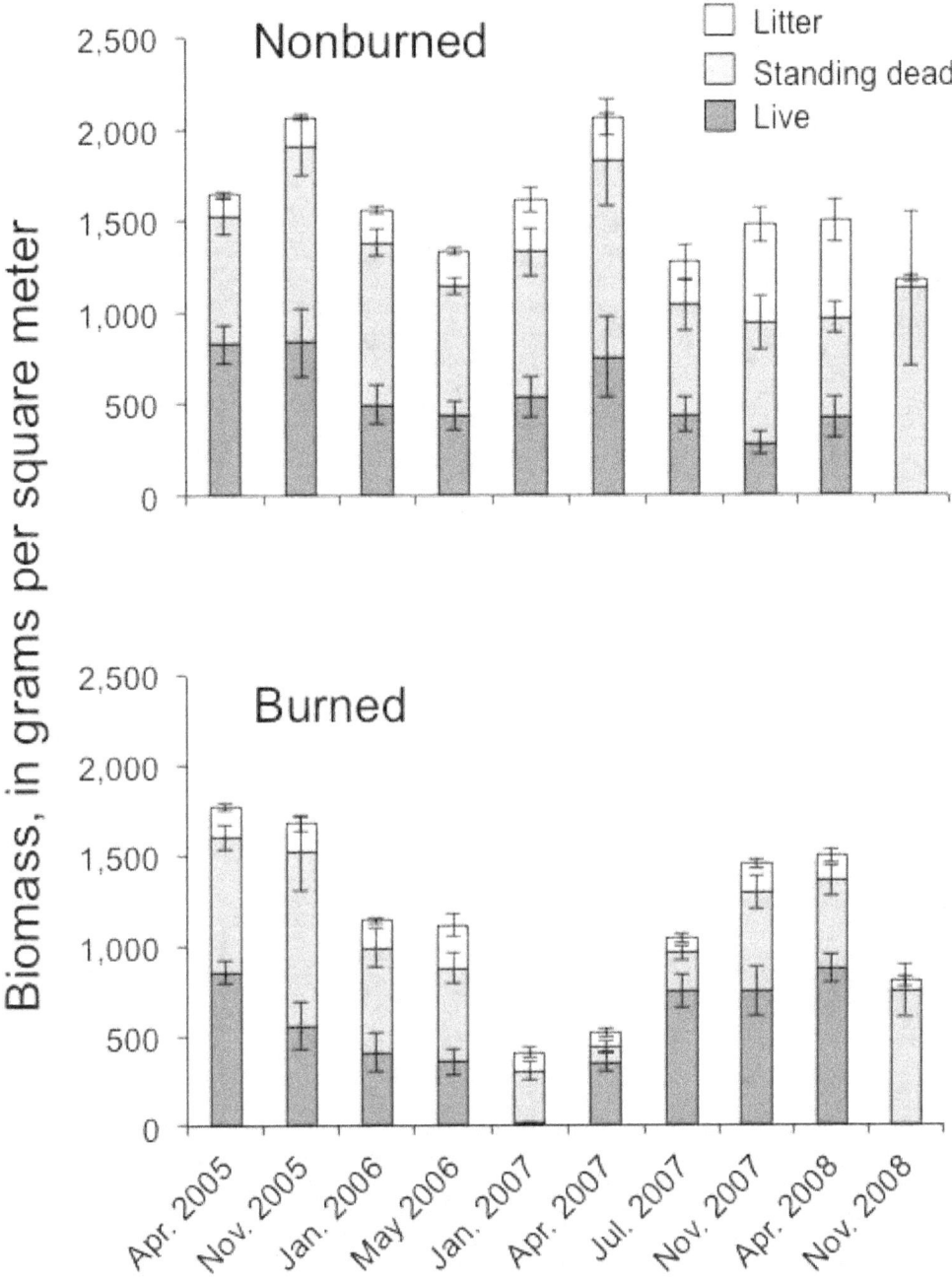

Figure 11. Standing live and dead biomass and fallen litter in burned and unburned plots (averaged over nutrient treatments; mean value ± standard error; n = 8). The prescribed burn occurred on December 3, 2006.

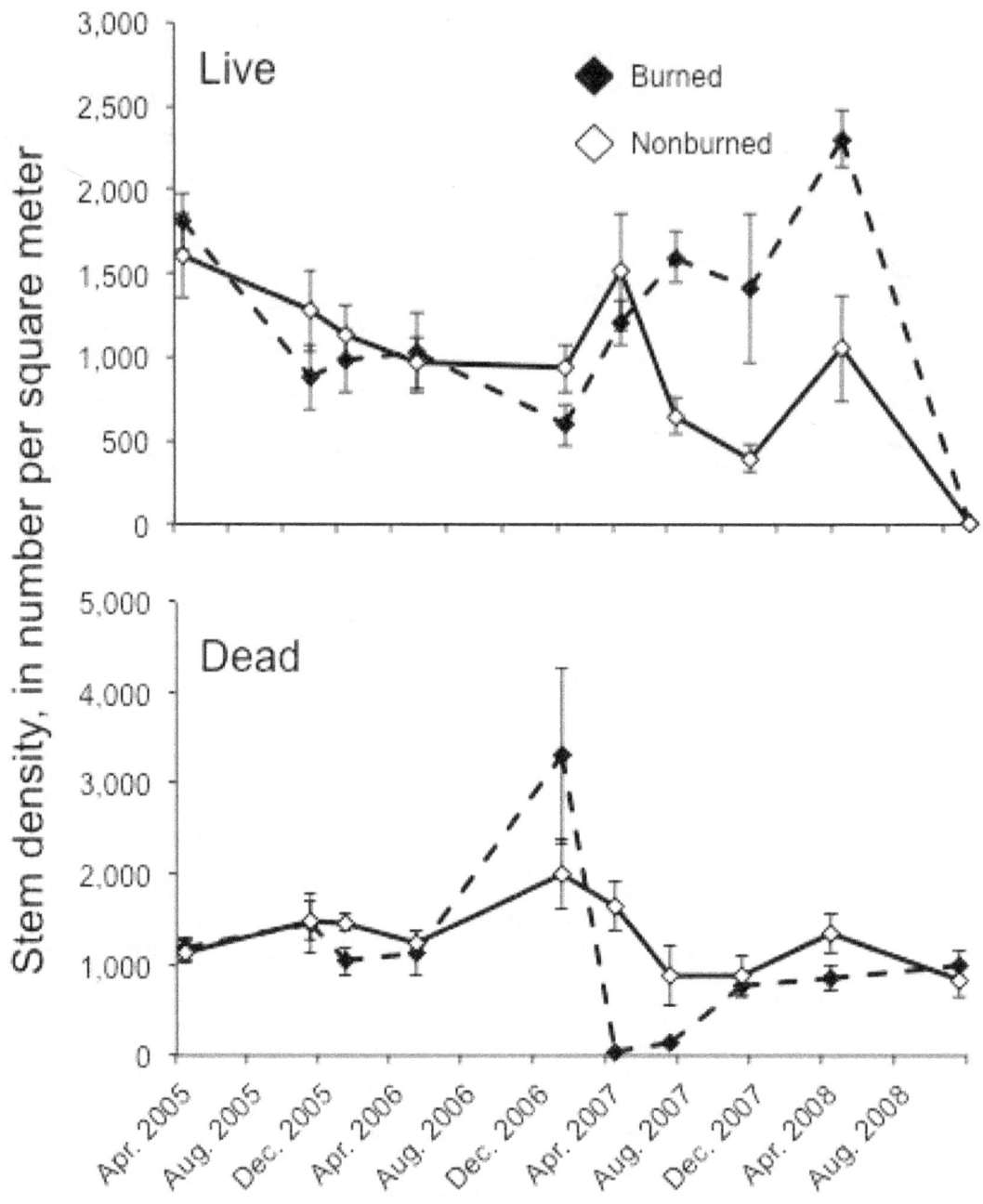

Figure 12. Variation in live and dead stem density in burned and nonburned plots (averaged over nutrient treatment; mean value ± standard error; n = 8,). The prescribed burn occurred on December 3, 2006.

These findings support one goal of prescribed burning, which is to reduce fuel loads, but the findings also show that standing stocks of dead material rapidly return to pre-burn levels (within 1–2 years). Consequently, more frequent burning may be necessary to maintain low amounts of litter. Storm surge from hurricanes may also reduce fuel loads by physically flushing out litter.

4. Result: Burning had no effect on aboveground or belowground production.

Burning may stimulate plant growth by rapidly mineralizing organic matter and adding nutrients or by removing standing and fallen dead litter and increasing light penetration to support new shoot growth. Although aboveground and belowground production rates varied annually, they were unaffected by the experimental treatments and averaged 1256 and 155 g m^{-2} yr^{-1}, respectively, across all plots and years (fig. 13). Belowground production varied significantly with depth; most root matter accumulated in the upper 10 cm (121 g m^{-2} yr^{-1}) compared to the deeper layers (16 – 19 g m^{-2} yr^{-1}).

At Blackwater NWR, annual burning increased both aboveground and belowground production (Cahoon et al. 2010). The lack of response at McFaddin NWR may be due to the lesser frequency of burn treatment, compared to that at Blackwater NWR. Another difference between the two studies is that the plant community at Blackwater NWR contained *Schoenoplectus americanus* in addition to *S. patens*, whereas the marsh at McFaddin NWR was dominated by a near-monoculture of *S. patens*. The two species differ in their responses to disturbance, and growth of *S. patens* may not be as responsive to burning as *S. americanus*. Another possibility is that annual burning removed more dead standing and fallen litter at Blackwater NWR, which promoted greater production of new shoots in spring.

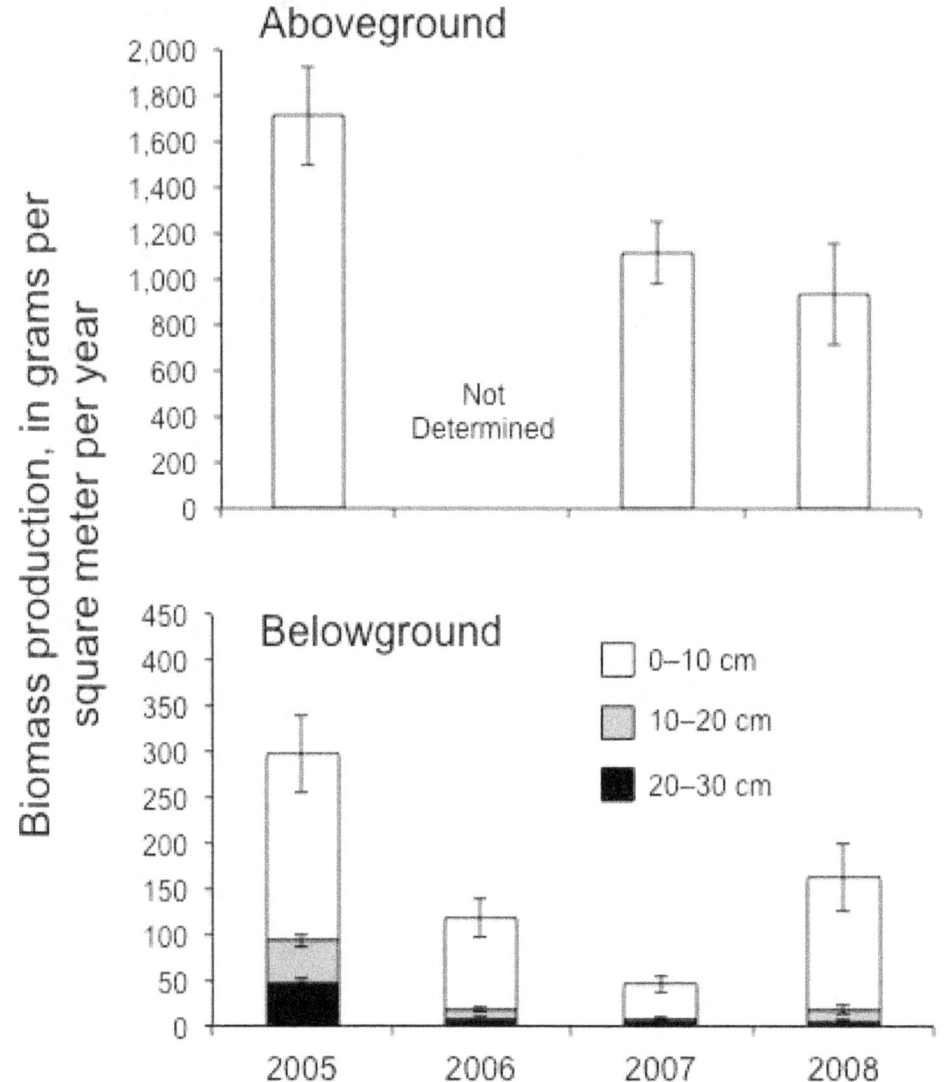

Figure 13. Aboveground and belowground production of biomass (averaged over burn and nutrient treatments; mean value ± standard error; n =8). The prescribed burn occurred on December 3, 2006.

5. Result: Decomposition in upper soil layers was increased by burning.

Accumulation of organic matter requires slower rates of decomposition than production. Burning may accelerate decomposition of soil organic matter by stimulating the activity of the soil microbial community via changes in nutrients or other environmental conditions. Burial of a standard cellulose material in the experimental plots allowed assessment of the decomposition potential—essentially the activity of the microbial community--at different soil depths within the root zone where most of the belowground production occurred.

Decomposition of the standard cellulose material (summer 2007) varied by soil depth (main effect, $P < 0.001$) and was faster in upper soil layers in burned plots (interaction of depth by fire, $P = 0.05$) (fig. 14). There was no effect of nutrient addition on tensile strength loss, suggesting that the effect of burning on decomposition was not related to changes in availability of nitrogen, phosphorus, and potassium. Although decomposition appeared to be stimulated in burned plots, the greater accretion above the marker horizon counterbalanced any losses in organic matter, so that the net effect was a greater gain in elevation. If there had been lower surface accretion at this site or higher subsidence rates, however, the increased rate of decomposition could have had a greater influence on elevation.

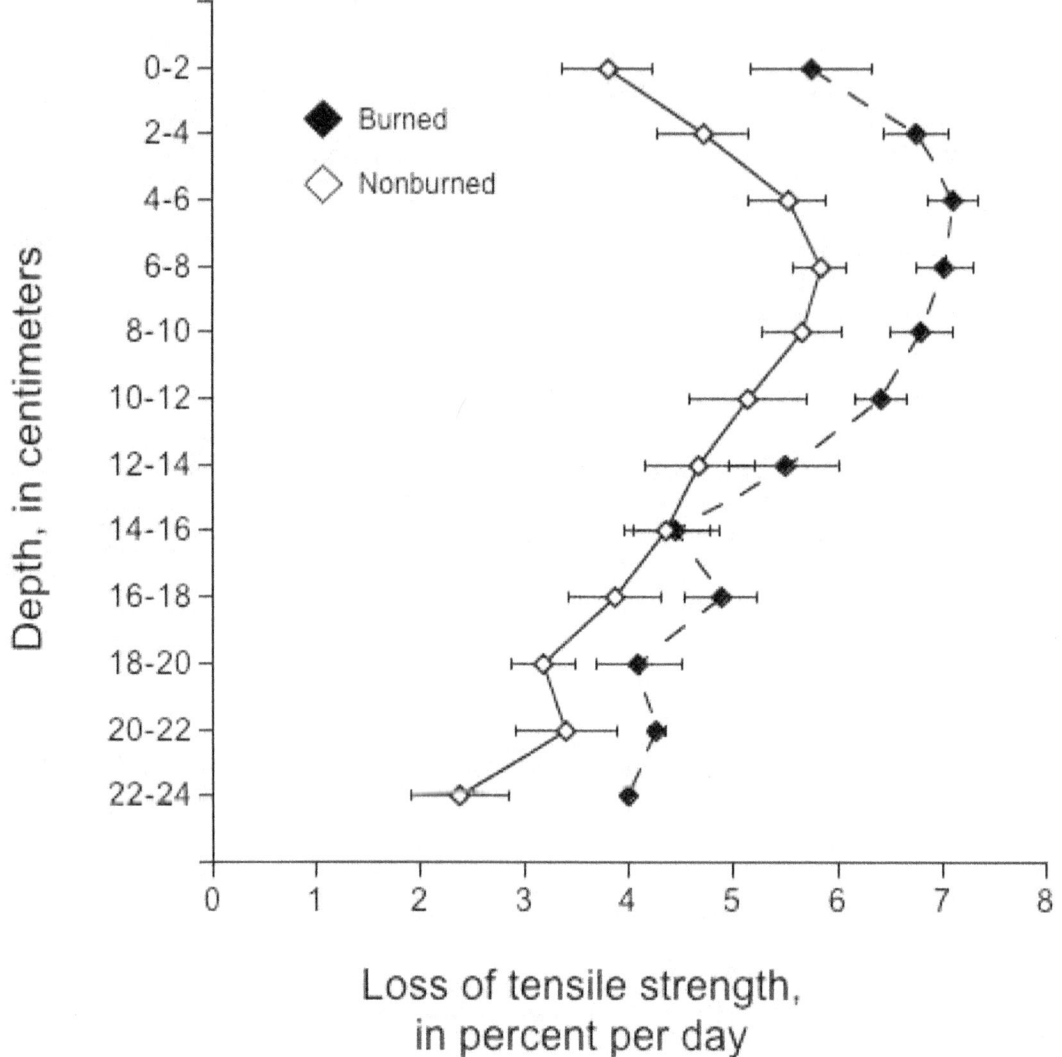

Figure 14. Depth variation in decomposition of standard cellulose material in burned and nonburned plots (summer of 2007) (averaged over nutrient treatment; mean value ± standard error; n = 8).

6. Result: Soil physicochemistry was unaffected by burning or nutrient addition.

Soil bulk density across all plots averaged 0.1 ± 0.01 grams per cubic centimeter ($g\ cm^{-3}$), and percent organic matter averaged 56 ± 2. There were no differences in these variables attributable to burning, nutrient addition, or season. Also, there were no substantial effects of either burning or nutrient treatments on soil or porewater chemistry, although these parameters varied significantly over time (fig. 15). Soil redox potential and sulfide concentration indicate flooding-related conditions and typically vary seasonally with soil flushing and plant growth. The levels measured during this study suggested low to moderate flooding stress at the study site, which increased over the period of observation. Salinity increased after Hurricane Ike, but values remained within the tolerance range of *S. patens*. Salinity was significantly higher in burned (11 parts per thousand [ppt]) versus nonburned (10 ppt) plots, but this difference was slight and not biologically significant. Porewater concentrations of nutrients (ammonium [NH_4] and phosphate [PO_4]) fluctuated seasonally and annually but did not show a significant response to treatments. Plant uptake and/or chemical transformations likely explain why porewater concentrations of these nutrients were not elevated in nutrient-amended plots.

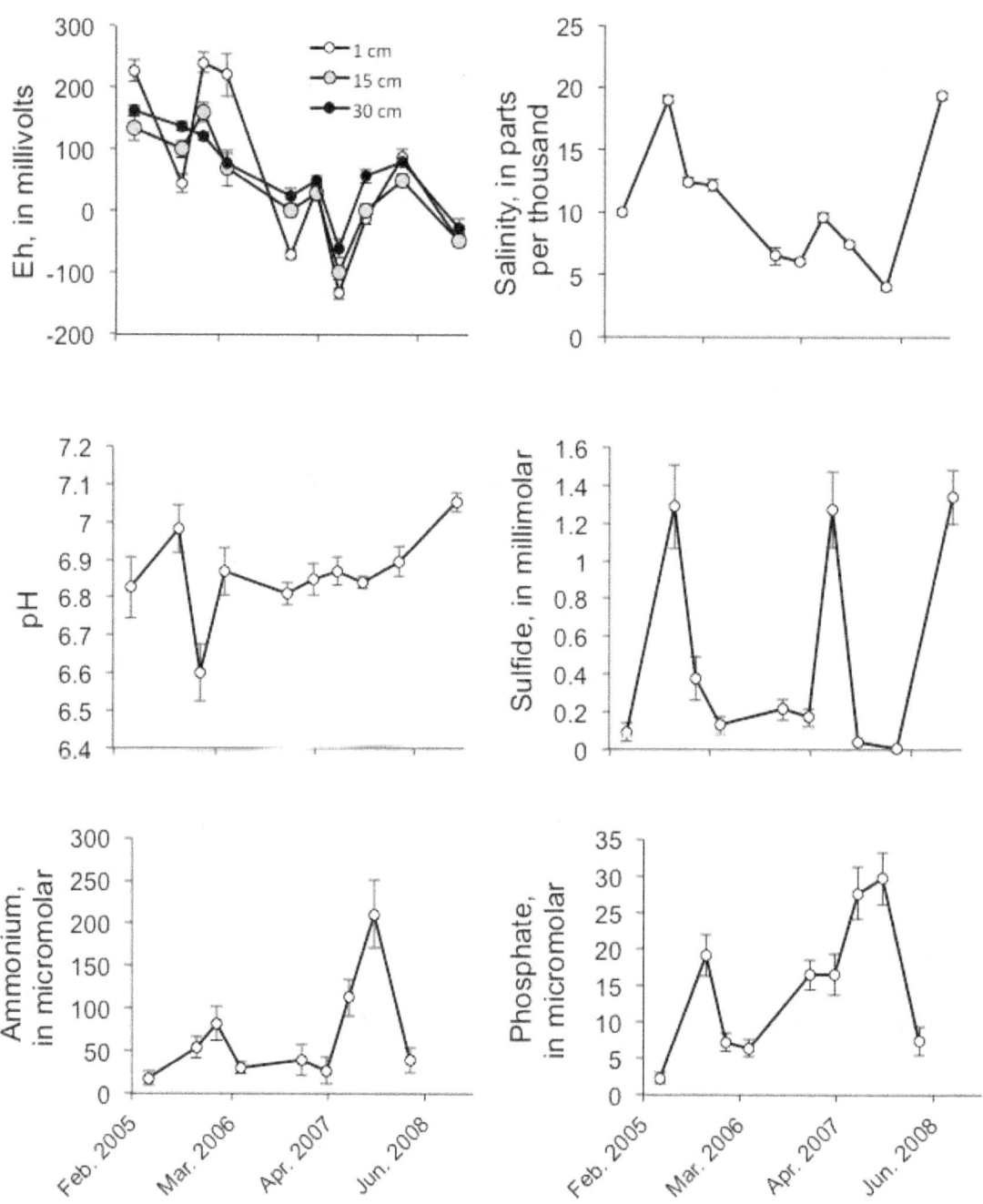

Figure 15. Soil redox potential (Eh) at soil depth (in centimeters) and porewater salinity, pH,

sulfide, ammonium (NH_4), and phosphate (PO_4) measured seasonally in experimental plots

(averaged over treatments; mean value ± standard error; n = 16).

7. **Result:** The elevation deficit was lower in burned plots (6.2 mm yr^{-1}) compared to nonburned plots (7.2 mm yr^{-1}).

The vulnerability of marshes to sea-level rise is determined by the rate of vertical marsh building relative to the rate of submergence, that is, relative SLR (table 2). The relative SLR for the region is based on measurements from local tide gages. In this case, mean sea level rise was estimated at 6.3 mm yr^{-1} (NOAA, 2011). This value reflects changes in water level as well as land movement below the base of the tide gage. To determine the true relative SLR, however, the rate of shallow subsidence (between the base of the tide gage and the land surface) must be added to the rate of relative SLR based on the tide gage. This value is provided by the SET measurements.

The subroot-zone movements were -4.6 mm yr^{-1} (burned plots) and -3.1 mm yr^{-1} (nonburned plots), giving a total submergence rate of 10.9 mm yr^{-1} and 9.4 mm yr^{-1}, respectively. To maintain soil elevations relative to submergence, land building must occur at equivalent rates. The rate of land building is the combination of root zone expansion plus accretion on the soil surface. The combined rates of gain prior to Hurricanes Gustav and Ike were 4.7 mm yr^{-1} (burned plots) and 2.2 mm yr^{-1} (nonburned plots). Thus, the elevation deficit was lower in the burned plots (6.2 mm yr^{-1}) compared to nonburned plots (7.2 mm yr^{-1}) prior to these hurricanes (main effect of fire, F = 5.41, P = 0.0484). Because storm sediments subsequently altered elevation dynamics at this site, it was not possible to determine how much longer this difference in elevation deficit would have been maintained.

Table 2. Summary of relative sea-level rise (SLR) and elevation dynamics in burned and nonburned plots at McFaddin National Wildlife Refuge prior to Hurricanes Gustav and Ike (September 2008). Values (in millimeters per year) are the mean value ± standard error.

	Burned	Nonburned
Relative SLR[1]	6.3	6.3
Sub-root zone subsidence	4.6 ± 2.2	3.1 ± 1.3
Total Submergence	**10.9 ± 2.2**	**9.4 ± 1.3**
Root zone expansion	0.2 ± 0.2	0.3 ± 0.1
Surface accretion	4.5 ± 0.5	1.9 ± 0.6
Total Land Building	**4.7 ± 0.5**	**2.2 ± 0.6**
Elevation Deficit[2]	**6.2 ± 2.0**	**7.2 ± 1.0**

[1]Relative SLR equals the change in mean sea level plus deep land movement (from tide gauge records) (NOAA, 2011).

[2] Elevation deficit equals total submergence minus total land building.

8. **Result:** Storm sediments delivered by Hurricanes Gustav and Ike raised elevations an average of 7.4 cm, which countered an elevation deficit accrued over the course of 11 years.

The study site exhibited an overall elevation deficit of 6.7 mm yr^{-1} from April 2005 to April 2008. In September 2008, 3 to 9 cm of sediment were deposited in plots, which raised elevations an average of 7.4 ± 0.9 cm (fig. 9). The bulk of this sediment was likely delivered by Hurricane Ike, based on storm surge heights for the area (East and others, 2008). This single event countered an elevation deficit accrued over the course of

11 years (estimated by dividing storm-induced elevation gain by an annual average deficit of 6.7 mm yr^{-1}). This finding was in contrast to Hurricane Rita, which did not deliver measurable sediment to study plots (fig. 9). A similar effect on elevation due to sediment input by Hurricane Katrina was found in subsiding brackish marshes in Louisiana (McKee and Cherry, 2009). Between 3 and 8 cm of sediment were added to the soil surface at Big Branch Marsh NWR and Pearl River Wildlife Management Area (WMA) during the storm surge. At those sites, where the submergence rate (mean relative SLR + subsidence) was 21 mm yr^{-1}, the hurricane sediment was important in countering elevation loss. Although the elevations measured after Hurricane Katrina continued to decline (because of continuing subsidence, root-zone collapse, and/or compaction of deposited sediment), net elevation gain was still positive two years later. In addition, belowground accumulation of root matter was stimulated 10-fold at Big Branch Marsh NWR, which further contributed to upward expansion of the soil surface.

In contrast to the above effects, marsh flooding caused by Tropical Storm Charley (August 1998) and Tropical Storm Frances (September 1998) led to plant dieback and soil collapse at McFaddin NWR (Cahoon and others, 2004). In that instance, floodwaters from the storm surge covered the marsh surface to a maximum depth of 1.5 m, and marshes remained flooded for about two months. Since the study by Cahoon et al. (2004) was initiated after floodwaters had receded, it is unknown how much sediment may have been deposited. The rate of accretion measured during the year following the storms, however, was 4 to 5 mm yr^{-1}, which was insufficient to counterbalance the rate of collapse (37 to 68 mm yr^{-1}).

The results of studies in Texas and Louisiana illustrate the potentially positive effects of storm sediment on elevation dynamics in coastal marshes. Although some coastal marshes may suffer collapse, erosion, or other negative impacts from hurricane disturbance, subsiding areas that receive sufficient sediment to alter elevation trajectories may benefit in the long-run. However, not all hurricanes will deliver sediment sufficient to alter accretion and elevation trajectories, as suggested by the differences between Hurricanes Ike and Rita. Additional monitoring of elevations at McFaddin NWR will be required to assess if sediments deposited by 2008 hurricanes might influence future elevation gain via stimulation of belowground production.

Conclusions

General Implications for Resource Management

1. Prescribed burning conducted at 3- to 5-year intervals does not seem to pose an additional risk to long-term sustainability of *S. patens*-dominated brackish marshes at McFaddin NWR.

The results of this cooperative study indicate that the current prescribed fire regime (3–5 year frequency) at McFaddin NWR seems to pose no additional threat to marsh sustainability and may offset existing elevation deficits by approximately 1 mm yr^{-1}. Although this specific offset cannot be extrapolated beyond the study period or to other coastal refuges, the findings at McFaddin NWR and Blackwater NWR together suggest that prescribed fire may provide benefits to future sustainability of *some* brackish marshes. The potential effect of burning on elevation change will depend on several site-specific factors, including geomorphic/sedimentary setting, tide range, local rate of relative SLR, plant species composition, additional management practices (e.g., for flood control), and disturbance types and frequency (for example, hurricanes and herbivore grazing). Sites undergoing high rates of subsidence and/or intense herbivory, for example, might be negatively affected by burning. Further studies conducted in different marsh types and hydroedaphic settings and at different burn intervals will be required for further understanding.

2. The primary drivers of elevation change vary in time and space, leading to a more complex situation in terms of predicting how disturbances may alter elevation trajectories.

A growing body of information suggests that various processes, both physical and biological, contribute to vertical movement in different soil layers. In this study, we partitioned movement in three main zones, including the soil surface (above a marker horizon), root zone, and subroot zone. Besides this study, two other studies have examined effects of movement in discrete strata on total elevation change in brackish marshes (McKee and Cherry, 2009; Cahoon and others, 2010). Movement in each of these strata is controlled by a different suite of processes and, consequently, may be influenced by different physical and biological drivers (fig. 16). Mineral sedimentation on the soil surface is influenced by tides and currents; by proximity to rivers, creeks and open ocean; by the composition of the sediment (particle-size distribution); by barriers to water movement; and by plant type and stem density (which baffles water movement). Expansion or contraction of the root zone is influenced by the growth cycle of the rooted vegetation, by factors influencing plant growth (nutrients, climate), and by factors influencing decomposition of organic matter. Subroot-zone movement is due to physical processes such as compaction (reduction in pore space) and by shrink-swell movement caused by surface and groundwater influx and steric changes in adjacent bays and oceans. Because these biophysical drivers may vary seasonally and/or annually and in response to stochastic events such as hurricanes, their relative influence also varies temporally. Also, the influence of seasonal or annual processes may obscure finer movements responsible for directional trends, making quantification of effects of burning and other management practices difficult to determine without long-term records (>5 years).

Research Implications

Long-term monitoring of elevation changes will provide additional insights into how processes controlling marsh elevations may change over time and how long elevation trajectories in burned plots will persist. The study sites at McFaddin NWR in Texas and Blackwater NWR in Maryland are the only two known locations where effects of prescribed fire on marsh-elevation dynamics have been evaluated. These two locations are very similar in that they are characterized by microtidal to nontidal astronomical ranges, are in subsiding geomorphic settings, and have low sediment supplies (during nonhurricane years). The McFaddin NWR site also provides a unique opportunity to follow long-term impacts of hurricane sedimentation on elevation dynamics. Together with sites such as those at the Big Branch Marsh NWR and the Pearl River WMA, the SET-instrumented plots represent a valuable resource that can continue to produce information in the future about hurricane effects on coastal marshes. To increase the scope of inference, SETs could be installed in replicate marshes undergoing different prescribed fire intervals and in different geomorphic settings (with different hurricane frequencies and/or different sedimentary settings). Multiple locations along the Gulf and

Atlantic coasts in which prescribed fire is used as a management tool would provide the

ideal setting for such installations.

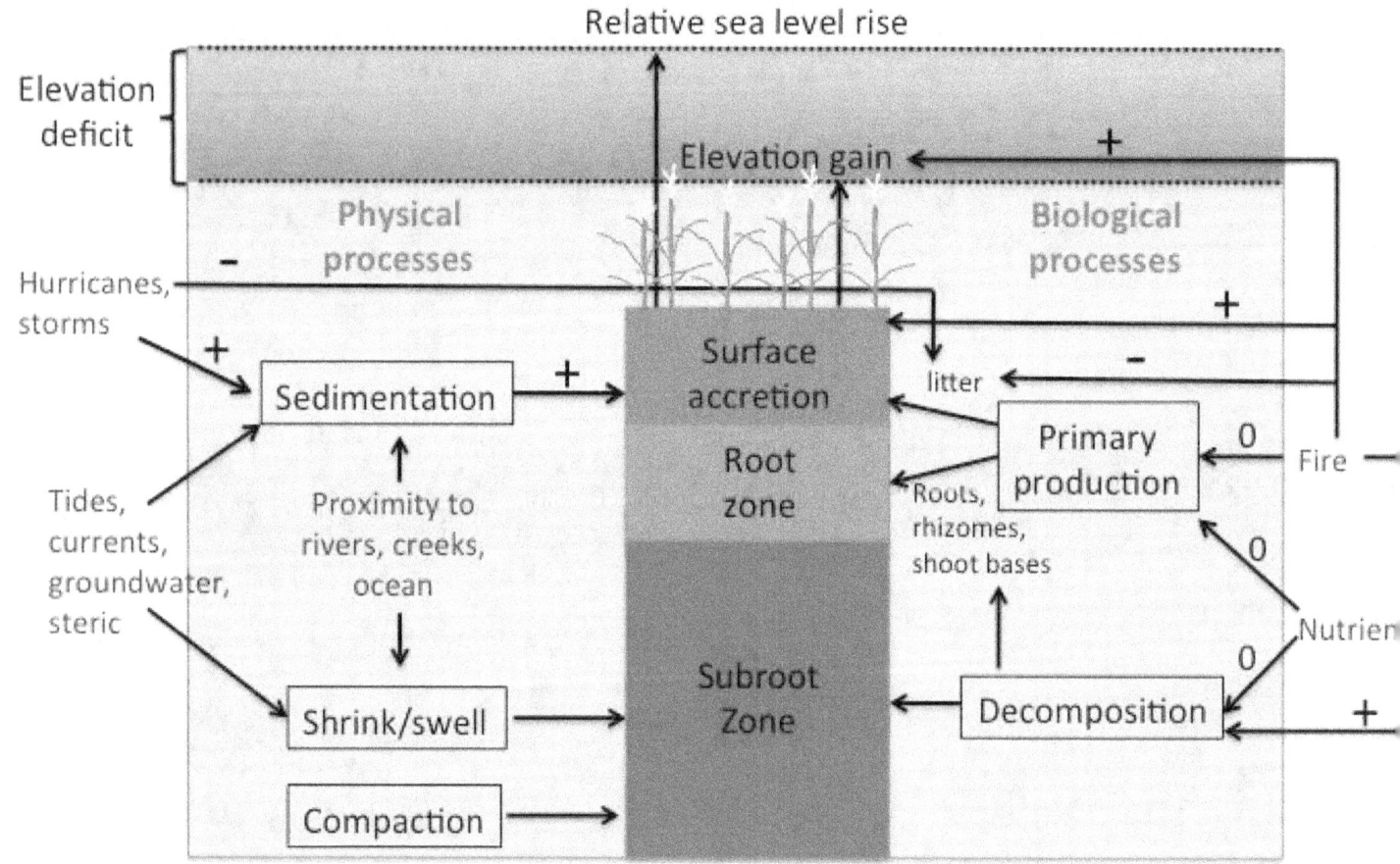

16. Conceptual model illustrating internal processes and external drivers influencing vertical movement in three soil strata in a b marsh dominated by *Spartina patens*, including accretion above a marker horizon, root zone, and subroot zone. Observed effects o nutrient addition, and hurricanes are indicated as follows: + (positive), - (negative), and 0 (none).

References Cited

Cahoon, D.R., Ford, M.A., and Hensel, P.F., 2004, Ecogeomorphology of *Spartina patens*-dominated tidal marshes: soil organic matter accumulation, marsh elevation dynamics, and disturbance, *in* Fagherazzi, Sergio, Marani, Marco, Blum, L.K., eds., The Ecogeomorphology of Tidal Marshes: Washington D.C., American Geophysical Union, p. 247-266.

Cahoon, D.R., Guntenspergen, G.R., Baird, Suzanne, Nagel, Jessica, Hensel, P. F., Lynch, J.C., Bishara, Dana, Brennand, Patrick, Jones, Joshua, and Otto, Clint, 2010, Do annual prescribed fires enhance or slow the loss of coastal marsh habitat at Blackwater National Wildlife Refuge? Final Project Report (JFSP Number 06-2-1-35), Final Project Report (JFSP Number 06-2-1-35): Beltsville, MD, p. 19 [http://www.firescience.gov/JFSP_Search_Results_Detail.cfm?jdbid=%24%26*%275V0%20%20%0A].

Cahoon, D.R., Lynch, J.C., and Knaus, R.M., 1996, Improved cryogenic coring device for sampling wetland soils: Journal of Sedimentary Research, v. 66, p. 1025-1027.

Cahoon, D.R., Lynch, J.C., Perez, B.C., Segura, Bradley, Holland, R.D., Stelly, Carroll, Stephenson, Gary, and Hensel, P.F., 2002, High-precision measurements of wetland sediment elevation: II. the rod surface elevation table: Journal of Sedimentary Research, v. 72, p. 734-739.

Cherry, J.A., McKee, K.L., and Grace, J.B., 2009, Elevated CO_2 enhances biological contributions to elevation change in coastal wetlands by offsetting stressors associated with sea-level rise Journal of Ecology, v. 97, p. 67-77.

East, J.W., Turco, M.J., and Mason Jr., R.R., 2008, Monitoring inland storm surge and flooding from Hurricane Ike in Texas and Louisiana, September 2008: U.S. Geological Survey Open-File Report 2008-1365, U.S. Geological Survey, [http://pubs.usgs.gov/of/2008/1365/].

Ford, M.A., and Grace, J.B., 1998, The interactive effects of fire and herbivory on a coastal marsh in Louisiana: Wetlands, v. 18, p. 1-8.

Gabrey, S.W., and Afton, A.D., 2001, Plant community composition and biomass in Gulf Coast chenier plain marshes: responses to winter burning and structural marsh management: Environmental Management, v. 27, p. 281-293.

Gauthier, Gilles, Hughes, R.J., Reed, Austin, Beaulieu, Julien, and Rochefort, Line, 1995, Effect of grazing by greater snow geese on the production of graminoids at an arctic site (Bylot Island, NWT, Canada): Journal of Ecology, v. 83, p. 653-664.

Guntenspergen, G.R., Cahoon, D.R., Grace, J.B., Steyer, G.D., Fournet, Stephen, Townson, M.A., and Foote, A.L., 1995, Disturbance and recovery of the Louisiana coastal marsh landscape from the impacts of Hurricane Andrew: Journal of Coastal Research, v. SI 21, p. 324-339.

Hackney, C.T., and De La Cruz, A.A., 1977, The ecology of a Mississippi tidal marsh: The effects of fire on the vegetation of a tidal marsh in St. Louis Bay, Mississippi, Mississippi Marine Resources Council, p. 23.

Langley, J.A., McKee, K.L., Cahoon, D.R., Cherry, J.A., and Megonigal, J.P., 2009, Elevated CO_2 stimulates marsh elevation gain, counterbalancing sea-level rise: Proceedings of the National Academy of Sciences, v. 106, p. 6182-6186.

McKee, K.L., 2011, Biophysical controls on accretion and elevation change in Caribbean mangrove ecosystems: Estuarine, Coastal and Shelf Science, v. 91, p. 475-483.

McKee, K.L., Cahoon, D.R., and Feller, I.C., 2007, Caribbean mangroves adjust to rising sea level through biotic controls on change in soil elevation: Global Ecology and Biogeography, v. 16, p. 545-556.

McKee, K.L., and Cherry, J.A., 2009, Hurricane Katrina sediment slowed elevation loss in subsiding brackish marshes of the Mississippi River Delta: Wetlands, v. 29, p. 2-15.

McKee, K.L., and McGinnis, T.E., 2002, Hurricane Mitch: Effects on mangrove soil characteristics and root contributions to soil stabilization: U.S. Geological Survey Open-File Report OFR-02-178, 64 p.

McKee, K.L., Mendelssohn, I.A., and Hester, M.W., 1988, Reexamination of pore water sulfide concentrations and redox potentials near the aerial roots of *Rhizophora mangle* and *Avicennia germinans*: American Journal of Botany, v. 75, p. 1352-1359.

Morris, J.T., 2007, Estimating net primary production of salt marsh macrophytes, *in* Fahey, T.J., Knapp, A.K., eds., Principles and standards for measuring primary production: New York, Oxford University Press, p. 106-119.

Morris, J.T., Sundareshwar, P.V., Nietch, C.T., Kjerfve, Bjorn, and Cahoon, D.R., 2002, Response of coastal wetlands to rising sea level: Ecology, v. 83, p. 2869-2877.

Mudd, S.M., Howell, S.M., and Morris, J.T., 2009, Impact of dynamic feedbacks between sedimentation, sea-level rise, and biomass production on near-surface marsh stratigraphy and carbon accumulation: Estuarine, Coastal and Shelf Science, v. 82, p. 377-389.

Neubauer, S.C., 2008, Contributions of mineral and organic components to tidal freshwater marsh accretion: Estuarine, Coastal and Shelf Science, v. 78, p. 78-88.

NOAA, n.d., Tides & Currents [http://www.tidesandcurrents.noaa.gov]: National Oceanic and Atmospheric Administration's National Ocean Service, accessed August 10, 2010, at http://www.tidesandcurrents.noaa.gov.

Nyman, J.A., and Chabreck, R.H., 1995, Fire in coastal marshes: history and recent concerns, *in* Cerulean, S.I., Engstrom, R.T., eds., Fire in wetlands: a management perspective, Proceedings of the tall timbers fire ecology conference No 19: Tallahassee, Fl., Tall Timbers Research Station, p. 134-141.

Nyman, J.A., DeLaune, R.D., Roberts, H.H., and Patrick Jr., W.H., 1993, Relationship between vegetation and soil formation in a rapidly submerging coastal marsh: Marine Ecology Progress Series, v. 96, p. 269-279.

Nyman, J.A., Walters, R.J., DeLaune, R.D., and Patrick Jr., W.H., 2006, Marsh vertical accretion via vegetative growth: Estuarine, Coastal and Shelf Science, v. 69, p. 370-380.

Parent, L.E., and Caron, Jean, 1993, Physical properties of organic soils, *in* Carter, M.R., ed. Soil Sampling and Methods of Analysis: Boca Raton, Lewis Publishers, p. 441-458.

Parry, M.L., Canziani, O.F., and Palutikof, J.P., 2007, Technical Summary, *in* Parry, M.L., Canziani, O.F., Palutikof, J.P., van der Linden, P.J., Hanson, C.E., eds., Climate Change 2007: Impacts, Adaptation and Vulnerability Contribution of

Working Group II to the Fourth Assessment Report of the Intergovernmental

Panel on Climate Change: Cambridge, UK, Cambridge University Press, p. 23-78.

Ponzio, K.J., Miller, S.J., and Lee, M.A., 2004, Long-term effects of prescribed fire on

Cladium jamaicense Crantz. and *Typha domingensis* Pers. densities: Wetlands

Ecology and Management, v. 12, p. 123-133.

Sanders, C.J., Smoak, J.M., Naidu, A.S., and Patchineelamt, S.R., 2008, Recent sediment

accumulation in a mangrove forest and its relevance to local sea-level rise (Ilha

Grande, Brazil): Journal of Coastal Research, v. 24, p. 533-536.

Schmalzer, P.A., Hinkle, C.R., and Mailander, J.L., 1991, Changes in community

composition and biomass in *Juncus roemerianus* Scheele and *Spartina bakeri*

Merr. marshes one year after a fire: Wetlands, v. 11, p. 67-86.

Silliman, B.R., van de Koppel, Johan, Bertness, M.D., Stanton, L.E., and Mendelssohn,

I.A., 2005, Drought, snails, and large-scale die-off of southern U.S. salt marshes:

Science, v. 310, p. 1803-1806.

Slocum, M.G., Roberts, Joshua, and Mendelssohn, I.A., 2009, Artist canvas as a new

standard for the cotton-strip assay: Journal of Plant Nutrition and Soil Science, v.

172, p. 71-74.

Smith, S.M., Newman, Sue, Garrett, P.B., and Leeds, J.A., 2001, Differential effects of

surface and peat fire on soil constituents in a degraded wetland of the Northern

Florida Everglades: Journal of Environmental Quality, v. 30, p. 1998-2005.

Turner, R.E., Milan, C.S., and Swenson, E.M., 2006, Recent volumetric changes in salt

marsh soils: Estuarine, Coastal and Shelf Science, v. 69, p. 352-359.

www.ingramcontent.com/pod-product-compliance
Lightning Source LLC
Chambersburg PA
CBHW080444290526
45791CB00008BA/2600